OUR BUCKET LIST

1. FIND SOUL MATE

Index

Index

When we decided to do this

_____

BUCKET LIST GOAL

WHY WE WANT TO DO IT

_____

_____

_____

_____

THINGS WE NEED TO PLAN

_____

_____

_____

_____

Date we actually did it

_____

RATING

BEST BITS

_____
_____
_____
_____

Our favourite picture

When we decided to do this

_____

BUCKET LIST GOAL

WHY WE WANT TO DO IT

_____
_____
_____
_____

THINGS WE NEED TO PLAN

_____
_____
_____
_____

Date we actually did it

RATING

BEST BITS

_____

_____

_____

_____

Our favourite picture

When we decided to do this

_____

BUCKET LIST GOAL

WHY WE WANT TO DO IT

_____
_____
_____
_____

THINGS WE NEED TO PLAN

_____
_____
_____

Date we actually did it

_____

RATING

BEST BITS

_____

_____

_____

_____

Our favourite picture

When we decided to do this

_____

>> BUCKET LIST GOAL <<

WHY WE WANT TO DO IT

_____
_____
_____
_____

THINGS WE NEED TO PLAN

_____
_____
_____
_____

Date we actually did it

_____

RATING

BEST BITS

_____
_____
_____
_____

Our favourite picture

When we decided to do this

BUCKET LIST GOAL

WHY WE WANT TO DO IT

THINGS WE NEED TO PLAN

Date we actually did it

_____

RATING

BEST BITS

_____
_____
_____
_____

Our favourite picture

When we decided to do this

_____

BUCKET LIST GOAL

WHY WE WANT TO DO IT

_____
_____
_____
_____

THINGS WE NEED TO PLAN

_____
_____
_____
_____

Date we actually did it

RATING 1 2 3 4 5

BEST BITS

_____

_____

_____

_____

Our favourite picture

When we decided to do this

_____

BUCKET LIST GOAL

WHY WE WANT TO DO IT

_____
_____
_____
_____

THINGS WE NEED TO PLAN

_____
_____
_____

Date we actually did it

_____

RATING

BEST BITS

_____

_____

_____

_____

Our favourite picture

When we decided to do this

_____

BUCKET LIST GOAL

WHY WE WANT TO DO IT

_____
_____
_____
_____

THINGS WE NEED TO PLAN

_____
_____
_____
_____

Date we actually did it

_____

RATING

Best bits

_____

_____

_____

_____

Our favourite picture

When we decided to do this

_____

Bucket list goal

WHY WE WANT TO DO IT

_____
_____
_____
_____

THINGS WE NEED TO PLAN

_____
_____
_____

Date we actually did it

_____

RATING

BEST BITS

_____
_____
_____
_____

Our favourite picture

When we decided to do this

_____

BUCKET LIST GOAL

WHY WE WANT TO DO IT

_____
_____
_____
_____

THINGS WE NEED TO PLAN

_____
_____
_____
_____

Date we actually did it

_____

RATING

BEST BITS

_____

_____

_____

_____

Our favourite picture

When we decided to do this

_____

BUCKET LIST GOAL

WHY WE WANT TO DO IT

_____
_____
_____
_____

THINGS WE NEED TO PLAN

_____
_____
_____
_____

Date we actually did it

RATING

BEST BITS

_____

_____

_____

_____

Our favourite picture

When we decided to do this

BUCKET LIST GOAL

WHY WE WANT TO DO IT

THINGS WE NEED TO PLAN

Date we actually did it

RATING

BEST BITS

Our favourite picture

When we decided to do this

BUCKET LIST GOAL

WHY WE WANT TO DO IT

_____

_____

_____

_____

THINGS WE NEED TO PLAN

_____

_____

_____

_____

Date we actually did it

RATING

BEST BITS

_____

_____

_____

_____

Our favourite picture

When we decided to do this

_____

BUCKET LIST GOAL

WHY WE WANT TO DO IT

_____
_____
_____
_____

THINGS WE NEED TO PLAN

_____
_____
_____
_____

Date we actually did it

_____

Rating

Best bits

_____

_____

_____

_____

Our favourite picture

When we decided to do this

_____

BUCKET LIST GOAL

WHY WE WANT TO DO IT

_____

_____

_____

_____

THINGS WE NEED TO PLAN

_____

_____

_____

_____

Date we actually did it

_____

RATING

BEST BITS

_____
_____
_____
_____

Our favourite picture

When we decided to do this

_____

BUCKET LIST GOAL

WHY WE WANT TO DO IT

_____

_____

_____

_____

THINGS WE NEED TO PLAN

_____

_____

_____

_____

Date we actually did it

_____

RATING

BEST BITS

_____
_____
_____
_____

Our favourite picture

When we decided to do this

BUCKET LIST GOAL

↓ ↓

WHY WE WANT TO DO IT

_____

_____

_____

_____

THINGS WE NEED TO PLAN

_____

_____

_____

_____

♡

Date we actually did it

RATING

BEST BITS

Our favourite picture

When we decided to do this

_____

BUCKET LIST GOAL

↓   ↓

WHY WE WANT TO DO IT

_____
_____
_____
_____

THINGS WE NEED TO PLAN

_____
_____
_____
_____

♡

Date we actually did it

Rating

Best bits

_____

_____

_____

_____

Our favourite picture

When we decided to do this

_____

BUCKET LIST GOAL

↓   ↓

WHY WE WANT TO DO IT

_____
_____
_____
_____

THINGS WE NEED TO PLAN

_____
_____
_____
_____

♡

Date we actually did it

RATING

BEST BITS

Our favourite picture

When we decided to do this

_____

BUCKET LIST GOAL

WHY WE WANT TO DO IT

_____

_____

_____

_____

THINGS WE NEED TO PLAN

_____

_____

_____

_____

Date we actually did it

RATING

BEST BITS

_____

_____

_____

_____

Our favourite picture

When we decided to do this

BUCKET LIST GOAL

↓ ↓

WHY WE WANT TO DO IT

_____

_____

_____

_____

THINGS WE NEED TO PLAN

_____

_____

_____

_____

♡

Date we actually did it

_____

Rating ★1 ★2 ★3 ★4 ★5

Best bits

_____
_____
_____
_____

Our favourite picture

When we decided to do this

BUCKET LIST GOAL

WHY WE WANT TO DO IT

_____

_____

_____

_____

THINGS WE NEED TO PLAN

_____

_____

_____

_____

Date we actually did it

_____

RATING

BEST BITS

_____
_____
_____
_____

Our favourite picture

When we decided to do this

BUCKET LIST GOAL

WHY WE WANT TO DO IT

_____
_____
_____
_____

THINGS WE NEED TO PLAN

_____
_____
_____
_____

Date we actually did it

RATING

BEST BITS

_____

_____

_____

_____

Our favourite picture

When we decided to do this

BUCKET LIST GOAL

↓   ↓

WHY WE WANT TO DO IT

_____
_____
_____
_____

THINGS WE NEED TO PLAN

_____
_____
_____
_____

♡

Date we actually did it

_____

RATING

BEST BITS

_____
_____
_____
_____

Our favourite picture

When we decided to do this

_____

BUCKET LIST GOAL

WHY WE WANT TO DO IT

_____

_____

_____

_____

THINGS WE NEED TO PLAN

_____

_____

_____

_____

Date we actually did it

_____

RATING

BEST BITS

_____
_____
_____
_____

Our favourite picture

When we decided to do this

_____

BUCKET LIST GOAL

↓ ↓

WHY WE WANT TO DO IT

_____

_____

_____

_____

THINGS WE NEED TO PLAN

_____

_____

_____

_____

♡

Date we actually did it

RATING

BEST BITS

Our favourite picture

When we decided to do this

_____

BUCKET LIST GOAL

↓   ↓

WHY WE WANT TO DO IT

_____
_____
_____
_____

THINGS WE NEED TO PLAN

_____
_____
_____
_____

♡

Date we actually did it

_____

Rating

Best bits

_____
_____
_____
_____

Our favourite picture

When we decided to do this

_____

BUCKET LIST GOAL

WHY WE WANT TO DO IT

_____
_____
_____
_____

THINGS WE NEED TO PLAN

_____
_____
_____
_____

Date we actually did it

RATING

BEST BITS

_____

_____

_____

_____

Our favourite picture

When we decided to do this

_____

BUCKET LIST GOAL

WHY WE WANT TO DO IT

_____

_____

_____

_____

THINGS WE NEED TO PLAN

_____

_____

_____

_____

Date we actually did it

_____

RATING

BEST BITS

_____

_____

_____

_____

Our favourite picture

When we decided to do this

_____

BUCKET LIST GOAL

↓ ↓

WHY WE WANT TO DO IT

_____
_____
_____
_____

THINGS WE NEED TO PLAN

_____
_____
_____
_____

Date we actually did it

RATING

BEST BITS

Our favourite picture

When we decided to do this

_____

BUCKET LIST GOAL

↓   ↓

WHY WE WANT TO DO IT

_____
_____
_____
_____

THINGS WE NEED TO PLAN

_____
_____
_____
_____

Date we actually did it

RATING

BEST BITS

_____

_____

_____

_____

Our favourite picture

When we decided to do this

_____

BUCKET LIST GOAL

↓   ↓

WHY WE WANT TO DO IT

_____
_____
_____
_____

THINGS WE NEED TO PLAN

_____
_____
_____

♡

Date we actually did it

RATING

BEST BITS

Our favourite picture

When we decided to do this

_____

BUCKET LIST GOAL

WHY WE WANT TO DO IT

_____
_____
_____
_____

THINGS WE NEED TO PLAN

_____
_____
_____

Date we actually did it

_____

RATING

BEST BITS

_____
_____
_____
_____

Our favourite picture

When we decided to do this

_____

BUCKET LIST GOAL

WHY WE WANT TO DO IT

_____
_____
_____
_____

THINGS WE NEED TO PLAN

_____
_____
_____

Date we actually did it

RATING

BEST BITS

_____

_____

_____

_____

Our favourite picture

When we decided to do this

_____

BUCKET LIST GOAL

WHY WE WANT TO DO IT

_____

_____

_____

_____

THINGS WE NEED TO PLAN

_____

_____

_____

_____

Date we actually did it

_____

RATING

BEST BITS

_____

_____

_____

_____

Our favourite picture

When we decided to do this

BUCKET LIST GOAL

↓   ↓

WHY WE WANT TO DO IT

_____

_____

_____

_____

THINGS WE NEED TO PLAN

_____

_____

_____

♡

Date we actually did it

RATING

BEST BITS

Our favourite picture

When we decided to do this

_____

BUCKET LIST GOAL

↓ ↓

WHY WE WANT TO DO IT

_____

_____

_____

_____

THINGS WE NEED TO PLAN

_____

_____

_____

_____

Date we actually did it

_____

RATING

BEST BITS

_____
_____
_____
_____

Our favourite picture

When we decided to do this

_____

BUCKET LIST GOAL

WHY WE WANT TO DO IT

_____
_____
_____
_____

THINGS WE NEED TO PLAN

_____
_____
_____
_____

Date we actually did it

RATING

BEST BITS

Our favourite picture

When we decided to do this

_____

BUCKET LIST GOAL

↓   ↓

WHY WE WANT TO DO IT

_____
_____
_____
_____

THINGS WE NEED TO PLAN

_____
_____
_____
_____

Date we actually did it

RATING

BEST BITS

Our favourite picture

When we decided to do this

_____

BUCKET LIST GOAL

↓   ↓

WHY WE WANT TO DO IT

_____
_____
_____
_____

THINGS WE NEED TO PLAN

_____
_____
_____
_____

♡

Date we actually did it

_____

Rating

Best bits

_____
_____
_____
_____

Our favourite picture

When we decided to do this

BUCKET LIST GOAL

↓   ↓

WHY WE WANT TO DO IT

_____

_____

_____

_____

THINGS WE NEED TO PLAN

_____

_____

_____

_____

♡

Date we actually did it

Rating

BEST BITS

Our favourite picture

When we decided to do this

_____

BUCKET LIST GOAL

WHY WE WANT TO DO IT

_____
_____
_____
_____

THINGS WE NEED TO PLAN

_____
_____
_____
_____

Date we actually did it

_____

RATING

BEST BITS

_____
_____
_____
_____

Our favourite picture

When we decided to do this

_____

BUCKET LIST GOAL

↓   ↓

WHY WE WANT TO DO IT

_____

_____

_____

_____

THINGS WE NEED TO PLAN

_____

_____

_____

♡

Date we actually did it

Rating

Best bits

_____

_____

_____

_____

Our favourite picture

When we decided to do this

_____

BUCKET LIST GOAL

↓   ↓

WHY WE WANT TO DO IT

_____
_____
_____
_____

THINGS WE NEED TO PLAN

_____
_____
_____
_____

♡

Date we actually did it

_____

Rating

Best bits

_____
_____
_____
_____

Our favourite picture

When we decided to do this

BUCKET LIST GOAL

WHY WE WANT TO DO IT

_____
_____
_____
_____

THINGS WE NEED TO PLAN

_____
_____
_____
_____

Date we actually did it

_____

RATING

BEST BITS

_____
_____
_____
_____

Our favourite picture

When we decided to do this

_____

BUCKET LIST GOAL

↓   ↓

WHY WE WANT TO DO IT

_____

_____

_____

_____

THINGS WE NEED TO PLAN

_____

_____

_____

Date we actually did it

RATING

BEST BITS

Our favourite picture

When we decided to do this

BUCKET LIST GOAL

WHY WE WANT TO DO IT

THINGS WE NEED TO PLAN

Date we actually did it

_____

Rating

Best bits

_____

_____

_____

_____

Our favourite picture

When we decided to do this

_____

BUCKET LIST GOAL

WHY WE WANT TO DO IT

_____
_____
_____
_____

THINGS WE NEED TO PLAN

_____
_____
_____
_____

Date we actually did it

_____

Rating

Best bits

_____

_____

_____

_____

_____

Our favourite picture

When we decided to do this

_____

BUCKET LIST GOAL

↓   ↓

WHY WE WANT TO DO IT

_____
_____
_____
_____

THINGS WE NEED TO PLAN

_____
_____
_____
_____

Date we actually did it

_____

RATING

BEST BITS

_____

_____

_____

_____

Our favourite picture

When we decided to do this

_____

BUCKET LIST GOAL

↓   ↓

WHY WE WANT TO DO IT

_____
_____
_____
_____

THINGS WE NEED TO PLAN

_____
_____
_____
_____

♡

Date we actually did it

RATING

BEST BITS

_____

_____

_____

_____

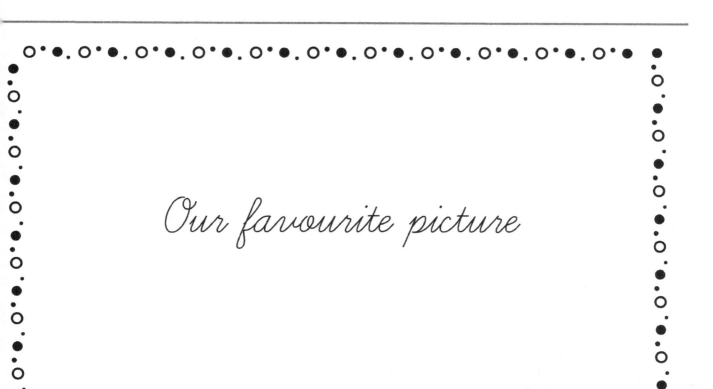

Our favourite picture

Made in the USA
Monee, IL
07 April 2021